Marti Angeloni

SO, HOW DO I KNOW THIS IS REAL?
by MARTI ANGELONI

Copyright ©2020 by Marti Angeloni

All rights reserved.

This book or part thereof may not be reproduced in any form by any means, electronic or mechanical, including photocopy, recording, or otherwise, or by any information storage and retrieval system, except as may be expressly permitted in writing from the publisher as provided by the United States of America copyright law. Requests for permission should be addressed to Doce Blant Publishing, Attn: Rights and Permissions Dept., 1600-B Dash Point Road, #1040, Federal Way, WA 98023

Published by
Doce Blant Publishing, Federal Way, WA, 98023
www.doceblantpublishing.com

Cover by Fiona Jayde Media
Interior Design by The Deliberate Page

Hardbound ISBN: 978-1-7344646-2-7
Paperback ISBN: 978-1-7344646-3-4
ePub ISBN: 978-1-7344646-4-1

Library of Congress Control Number: 2020930392

Printed in the United States of America

www.doceblant.com

This book is published for the sole purpose to provide information to readers with the understanding that the author and/or publisher is not engaged to render any type of psychological, legal, or any other type professional advice. The information and personal stories provided are the sole expression and opinion of the author, and not necessarily that of the publisher. No warranties or guarantees are expressed or implied. Although the author and publisher have made every effort to ensure that the information in this book was correct at press time, the author and publisher do not assume and hereby disclaim any liability to any party for any loss, damage, or disruption caused by errors or omissions, whether such errors or omissions result from negligence, accident, or any other cause. You are responsible for your own choices, actions, and results.

PREFACE

I NEVER CONSIDERED MYSELF GIFTED or blessed with "the shine," as many know it. So, looking for the metaphysical wasn't on my agenda. Yet, it kept cropping up—an unexplained love of graveyards and the history buried there, hearing my grandfather call out my name (he passed when I was eight), smelling my grandmother's unique blend of "J." hand cream and a chlorine cleanser, knowing what the patients assigned to me had going on health-wise just by looking at them. The list goes on and on.

This isn't strange to many reading this book. In fact, I suspect many of you have experienced similar, unexplained spiritual events in your life. These occurrences are typically viewed as coincidences—a phenomenon you'll soon realize does not exist, in my humble opinion.

After many years of dismissing these types of events, I finally couldn't ignore the presence of spiritual influence in life any longer—particularly after a dear friend and gifted medium called me out.

"How long have you been doing this?"

I gave her that look. "What are you talking about?"

"You know darn well. How long have you been spiritually gifted?"

My jaw hit the floor. "I'm not."

She smiled that *you just won't admit to it yet* smile and mercifully changed the subject. Still, I was intrigued and wanted to know more about what she saw in me, as well as understand her definition of "spiritually gifted."

This began a journey that brought me to self-reflection, admitting to events (like the ones described above), and eventual acceptance—all of this in answer to the most pressing question I had:

So, how do I know this is real?

CHAPTER 1
It Began with a Dream

I THINK I'LL PICK THE witches tonight.

I knew I'd end up in bed with my parents—that's the way it always went. Too afraid to stay in my own bed, my 5-year-old legs would run as fast as they could down the dark hallway and into my parents' bedroom. Mom usually let me cuddle with her for a few minutes before shooing me back to my own room.

Then the dream would begin again. Witches. Dark and scary, and out to get me. It was the same dream every time, nothing changed as I relived over and over again the gathering of witches coming forward toward me, their intent malevolent.

But the witches were better than the fire dream. I'd been having that one for the past week. Burning in a fire, unable to escape, unable to breathe. I never felt anything but the terror—the terror of being burned alive. That particular night, I couldn't take it anymore, so I chose the witches just for a break.

Each night, I would choose what my dreams would be. I was only a child, but I knew the choice was limited to the two that terrified me most. Infrequently, there would be an occasional night that the dreams didn't come. Those nights were peaceful and empty of any thoughts, images, or terror. Those nights were few but gratefully welcomed.

This lasted about three years—until I turned eight.

It seems that the above scenario, while belonging to me, is common with those who have the "gift" of tapping into the metaphysical. Many have told me that my dreams are memories of a past life coming through. Perhaps. Rather than analyze it, my decision was to acknowledge and accept it—to also accept that I wasn't crazy. That was the most important.

I suspect that same feeling has swept through many other "intuitives" who have experienced those same types of dreams, over and over again. In fact, almost everyone has experienced *that one dream* that seems to recur, unchanged. It grabs our attention often leaving us feeling a little unhinged.

The experts agree that repetitive dreams suggest the dreamer has unresolved life issues. Perhaps it's something that has caused stress or a nagging concern that needs your attention. Perhaps it's "a bit of undigested beef," as Scrooge would suggest. Most likely, it is memory stored deep within the dreamer's soul—indeed, begging to be noticed and acknowledged.

Whatever the cause, the dream is a reminder that you have business to attend to. Emotional problems, even contention between people in our lives, can create a negative energy that lingers. This negativity, even if temporarily forgotten, hovers in our subconscious and sucks the peace from our spirits.

A simple reflection of grudges, unfinished matters, family feuds, or bad feelings about someone can really backfire, leaving us with a deepening chasm that can't be ignored. As we move forward on our quest to combat anxiety, depression, and frustration in life, these negative influences block our progress.

Dreams remind us that we need to stop—to deal with the issue before we can move on. Dreams are like a neon sticky note from the sub-conscious. Avoiding them won't make them go away.

Repetitive dreams can have a deeper meaning for many. PTSD (post-traumatic stress disorder) is real and leaves an indelible mark on many. The trauma can be experienced in various forms, leaving a dark, bitter wake in its path. If ignored, the consequences of PTSD can be debilitating and overwhelming, often leading to serious consequences.

SO, HOW DO I KNOW THIS IS REAL?

These "stuffed issues" do not go away on their own. Rather, like a deep abscess, the emotional wounds fester and tunnel and spread throughout our souls until our spirit becomes septic, facing possible irreversible damage.

We cannot ignore these messages.

Let's consider the possibility of past life trauma. For those who don't hold with the concept of past lives, just go with this as a hypothesis for a moment. What if the medium was correct when she told me my dreams were of a past life? How would that affect my five-year-old self?

It is well-documented that terrifying trauma triggers the symptoms associated with PTSD. The event happens. Not everyone is affected the same—some not at all. The experience is individual and is a physiological response to a perceived threat from a previous event. Because each individual experiencing the event responds differently, it's easy to sit on the outside as an observer and think, *That didn't really happen* and *You're making it up*. Like feeling physical pain, the experience is personal and subjective. Each individual experiences the event differently but that does not eliminate its tangibility. To each person that experienced the trauma, the event is very authentic.

It is real.

Consider, for a moment, a trauma experienced by a woman in the 17th century as she is accused of witchcraft and then burned at the stake. Her death comes painfully, horrifically, and slowly. Once her spirit leaves her body, she moves into a place of peace and is able to recover from the experiences of life. Let's suppose she takes her memories with her. She holds on to the love and joy in life she has experienced. Her intelligence stays intact with her into the afterlife.

This makes sense and is confirmed by those who have experienced near-death events.

Going further into this scenario, what if she also retains memories from the last moments of her life? The last recollection of her life: rope chafing her bound wrists and ankles, looking down at the anger on the faces of onlookers, feeing sudden terror as the kindling is ignited, witnessing excruciating pain as her body burns to death until that merciful moment when her spirit abandons the flesh and climbs to another realm. It's an event that few can fathom.

Could this leave a PTSD memory within her soul?

Now, jump ahead to the 21st century. This same spirit has returned to a new life as a little girl living in suburban U.S.A. At night, the symptoms of PTSD haunt her as nightmares of burning alive. The likelihood of a young 5-year-old witnessing the execution of a witch in this manner is slim, at best. But the dreams come from somewhere. Her little mind has not been exposed to such horror in films or TV shows or books at this point. So, where do these vivid dreams come from?

There are many who would say these types of dreams are symptoms of past life PTSD. In fact, psychologists in Iceland, who study this phenomenon, state that children who report dreams of violent deaths may be exhibiting PTSD resulting from memories of past lives, often their own death. Many times, the child reports their memory in third person—an observer watching the violence playing out. Occasionally (as was my case), the child is the one experiencing the horrific event. In nearly every case, the child suffered PTSD-type symptoms.

Many of these children have difficulty sleeping and/or concentrating. Some have hyper-exaggerated startle responses. Others, exhibit anger or aggression when compared with children of their same age. Almost all are described as having "wild imaginations."

While my history does not include hyper-exaggerated startle responses or anger and aggression, I do suffer from disturbed sleep patterns (and as a fiction novel and screenwriter, the wild imagination thing certainly applies). In an evaluation of why I have trouble sleeping, my go-to response has been to attribute my stressful sleep to many years working the night shift as an RN. Graveyard shifts definitely disrupt circadian patterns over time. However, in reflection, the pattern of interrupted sleep occurred well before my years working in the medical field. I cannot attribute any specific cause for this and draw to, as one of my earliest childhood memories, these dreams as the beginning of sleepless nights.

It's a coincidence that I no longer believe is happenstance.

Suffering from repetitive dreaming (or not) isn't an indicator that you have had a past life event. The theory of past lives is merely an explanation for repetitive dreams and the possible resulting PTSD. To assign an absolute truth to such theory would be ridiculous. At this point, one can only hypothesize.

But the evidence supporting past life theory is real.

My dream occurrence was very real and continues to haunt me nearly 55 years later. From my experience, I have learned that acceptance of the event (a repetitive dream resulting from past life events) brings peace. In some instances, acceptance of this theory halted the repetition and eliminated the pattern. From a past life perspective, understanding that this is part of your history that must be acknowledged (as painful or terrifying as it is) helps to begin the healing process that needs to take place.

Non-judgement with any aspect of our history allows us to take a closer look at why the event happened. I will expand on this a little later in the book. For now, find your peace in knowing that there may be an explanation for the repetitive dreams that haunt you. Understand that if you exhibit signs and symptoms of PTSD, there is professional help available to you.

Suffering often comes from a form of self-judgement. PTSD and dream disturbance are events we are not meant to suffer from but rather, to understand, accept as real, and prohibit these occurrences to define or control our well-being.

WHY DOES THIS MATTER TO ME?

Dreams are real and have meaning. We're not crazy to admit that dreams seeming "so real" actually might have come from another lifetime. They're not meant to be brushed off or ignored. Messages are hidden within dreams—perhaps a life-lesson, a warning, reassurance, validation or communication from loved ones passed on. Perhaps, it's a memory.

But you're not crazy for having vivid, lucid dreams. Neither am I.

Life is meant to teach us. Dreams are a part of that learning experience. May we all be blessed with sweet dreams and greater insight.

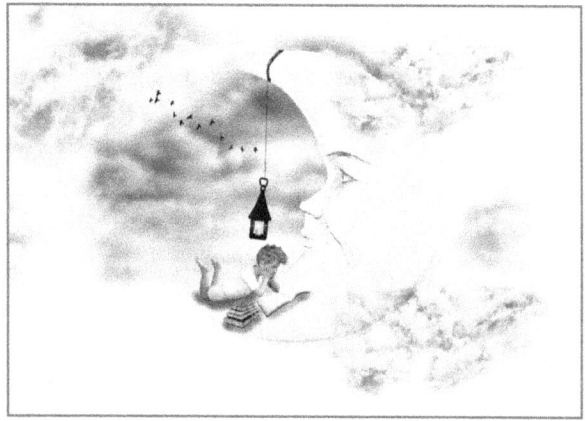

CHAPTER 2
Empathic Empathy or Why Being Told "You're too sensitive!" Still Hurts My Feelings

TEARS DAPPLED MY CHEEKS. I could barely keep my composure, even though the others were laughing, some even cheering.

"Batter up!" The umpire made the signal and another young man stepped up to home plate, swinging a bat menacingly.

"She'll be okay." The lady sitting next to me smiled that *you know how it is* smile and turned her attention back to the game. A crack sounded as the bat made contact with the ball and the lady leapt to her feet, arms up, screaming with the rest of the adults on the bleachers.

I glanced at the little girl sitting next to her. Her head was bowed. Lifting a sleeve to her nose, she swiped it and sniffed again. My heart pained again, and I felt the tears well up again. I sensed her pain. Try as I might, I couldn't pull my attention back to the game—I couldn't shake the sadness I knew was hers. My gut wrenched and I knew it would be a long night of sadness for that little girl...for me too.

Feelings matter.

It's called empathy and what sets us apart from narcists and sociopaths. The gift of empathy is cherished, especially by those who suffer and reap the benefits of another's compassion as a result. For those with deep, spiritual empathy, it can be both a blessing and a curse. Let me explain what I mean by first assigning a name to the individual who is gifted with deep-rooted empathy (disclaimer: I did not coin the moniker—this is a title well-understood in the psychological and metaphysical societies, respectively).

These people are called, "Empaths."

As an empath, it's nearly impossible to be near someone and not feel the same emotions as that person. In fact, most empaths *experience* the same emotions as others within their immediate proximity. Gifted with a heightened sensitivity to living beings, an empath senses the emotions, feelings, and even physical symptoms of another human being (animals included). It's a *knowing* about a person that cannot be explained. Many times, the *emotional sense* an empath experiences cannot be put into words—he just *knows*.

Why is this important?

Empathy is something we all strive to achieve—it shows we care and are genuinely sensitive to the needs of others. Those without empathy are often called, "cold" and "heartless," or the clinical designation of alexithymic. To be empathetic is a valued trait, often confused with sympathy.

These are not the same attributes.

To be sympathetic, one *shares* the feelings of another. To be empathetic, one *understands* the feelings of another. Both terms come from the Greek root word, pathos, which means:

The evocation of compassion or pity (Miriam Webster).

Sympathetic people tend to share feelings with others. Typically, this is associated with misfortune or pain. Empathetic people project another person's feelings onto themselves. Meaning, the empathic person *knows* or understands how a person feels, even though he may not overtly experience the same feeling.

On the surface, it would seem that sympathy is a more difficult trait to experience. Sharing pain or grief is difficult at best (hence, the massive availability of sympathy cards and flower arrangements).

SO, HOW DO I KNOW THIS IS REAL?

We make the effort to "share our sympathy" with those we recognize as suffering.

However, the exact opposite is true for an "empath."

Empaths take sentiments to an emotional warp speed. Beyond just feeling empathetic, an empath experiences emotion at a deep *knowing*, as if he is the person originating the feelings. But he is not. This causes tremendous pain at times for a true empath, requiring tremendous effort to balance the ever-churning onslaught of feelings that radiate from everyone around him. This makes empaths extremely vulnerable to depression, anxiety, and fearful reaction.

Even so, empaths are brilliant at hiding their gifts. It's a survival technique employed by nearly every empath. Some, while keenly aware of the heightened emotions they carry, remain unaware of the cause. Too often, these highly perceptive individuals are often dismissed as "overly-sensitive." Thus, begins the process of stuffing feelings and layering masks of happy-go-lucky faces to hide what lies brewing deep within. It's a grueling process.

Still, it's relatively easy to spot an empath—especially in public. Most true empaths eventually disappear in social gatherings, even small ones. Often tucked away somewhere unnoticed to embrace a moment of solitude, the empath seeks refuge in seclusion. Doing so alleviates some of the massive emotional download experienced in public spaces. It's the only way to regroup and begin the process of socializing again.

Methods exist to shield an empath—techniques to protect her from the onslaught of emotions arising from an association with others. These are tools that are frequently taught by spiritual mentors experienced in working with empaths. Use of light, crystals, prayer, water, and divine intervention are common for shielding. Suffice it to say, the empath is not helpless. In fact, she is very powerful, and her influence is profound.

So, why is a discussion about empaths important? I believe, empathic capability is the foundation for spirituality. I also believe nearly everyone has this gift. It begins as an emotional "gut-feeling."

We have all experienced it—that internal radar system that is driven by "a knot in the stomach" or "a bad feeling about this" or "there's such a great energy here" or "I've a gut feeling about that," etc. All of these are common phrases expressed about a physiologic event that senses something. Everyone experiences this "gut feeling" differently, however.

The degree each empath recognizes or utilizes his ability to know another person's emotional state is as diverse as each empath's personality and eye color. As human beings, we're individually different. That's obvious! So, naturally, our understanding and exploration of empathic ability will be different.

Our gifts will be different too.

Each of us have a natural predilection for a specific type of empathic ability. It's akin to playing an instrument—some play guitar while others play the lute. Similar but different—both provide music.

It is the same for empathic ability.

Without going into detail about each variety, a general description of several "types" of empath follows:

- **Emotional empaths** – this is the most commonly associated with the term "empath" and is linked with emotions and feelings. These empaths are gifted with the ability to easily sense the emotions of others. These individuals deeply experience the feelings of another person, as if those feelings were their own. The challenge is to identify which emotion belongs to whom. A frequent "check-in" with self to identify whether the emotion belongs to the empath or his neighbor is a good idea, especially in public settings.

- **Physical or medical empaths** – these individuals can literally feel an illness or injury suffered by another. The phrase, "He suffers from sympathy pains" comes from empathic sharing of physiologic conditions. On the occasion that the empath does not physically experience the same pain as another individual, he may *sense* it instead. This awareness may present unique challenges if not kept in check. As with every other empathic gift, it is imperative to know how to shield oneself and/or receive healing when needed.

- **Nature empath** – an empath who feels a strong connection to animals or plants will fall into this category. She will *know* what is needed and felt by animals. The same will be true for those who sense the needs of plant life. Generally, these empaths are found working in careers that keeps them close to that with which they connect (i.e.: an animal hospital or nature reserve). It is not necessary to connect with both animal *and* plant life to be considered a nature empath, nor is it required to be connected to *all* plants and/or *all* animals. The knowing happens when the empath is able to sense (possibly "hear") the needs of nature.

- **Environmental empath (also called Geomantic empaths)** – these gifted people have the ability to sense the environment. This goes beyond just plants, animals, objects and people. These empaths sense the tone of a location. This can expand to a sense of Mother Earth and the suffering of our world. If you are with someone who is uncomfortable with his surroundings, that person is likely an empath. Feng Shui has a direct effect on an environmental empath. It would not be surprising to find an environmental empath with a perfectly arranged living environment tuned into their own emotional needs.

- **Intuitive empath** – this gifted individual has the ability to sense a person's state of being just by being near. This gift is also known as Clair-cognizance and is used by many mediums when performing readings for individuals. An intuitive empath will know if someone is telling the truth, struggling financially, in an abusive relationship, or on the ladder to success.

They just *know*.

It is not uncommon for empaths to be gifted with more than one type of empathic ability. Frequently, an empath is not aware that they are gifted because they've "always been like this."

SO, WHY DOES THIS MATTER TO ME?

For as long as I can remember, I would hear my friends and family say, "You're just so sensitive!"

That stung.

Mostly, the cringe I felt inside when someone told me I was "too sensitive" happened because I associated that label with being pathetic or weak. My heart ached but my stubbornness wouldn't let anyone see it. I never wanted to be seen as fragile! Sensitive people are weak, or so I thought.

Jump ahead 50+ years and I realize I couldn't have been more incorrect in my assumption.

Always, I have felt deeply that just about anything has a living soul. Animals tend to get me the most, then nature, and finally people. My keen sense of knowing a person's heart is described as a gift of discernment. That is true. It also makes me an empath.

The moment I stopped thinking I was "too sensitive" and started trusting my intuition, I stopped making bad decisions. It's a crazy thought—listen to your intuition and you'll rarely stumble on the path of life.

That's a fact.

When you choose to pay attention to that *sense* of what a situation is or how a person (or animal) feels, you will find that your instinct about those things is right on! Trust follows on the heels of listening to your "gut feelings." Once that happens, you find that your inner

SO, HOW DO I KNOW THIS IS REAL?

compass rarely (I want to say "never" but was taught that absolutes are inappropriate in statements, generally...so just *know* that's what I mean) leads you astray.

This matters because it's a way to be "right" about your life path, attune to others' needs, in-tune to nature, and finally, live in peace.

Think about that for a minute...then listen to your "gut."

CHAPTER 3
Auras (You've got that outer glow!)

Today was my day to ship books and run errands. That meant a day spent at the U.S. Post Office. As I stood in the usual, long, daunting line, waiting to take my turn at the counter, my eyes began to wander. It would be unbearable if I couldn't find something to occupy the time while standing there. I started counting how many people were ahead of me (a lot!). When I hit the double-digits, I felt my spirits begin to sour...

...and then I saw her.

She stood patiently, dressed in a matching cap and coat the color of melted caramel. Her posture purported a dancer's background, and the gentle expression of her face imbued peace. I watched her for a while, admiring her, when I noticed a pale halo over her head, tipped in gold. I knew what it was, of course, but remained fascinated that her aura would shine so brightly amidst the chaos and irritability found in the post office.

I looked back to the counter, curious to see if anyone had moved away from it. Standing behind a metal divider, the postal worker beamed. Not just his smile, but his entire body had that same glow. His aura shown bigger and much more active than the lady's. Above his head, white light rose higher and higher—as if steam lifted from the crown of his head. Its buoyancy matched his joy.

Today is aura day.

The thought warmed my heart and suddenly, I didn't mind the long line as much. A chance to witness an aura is truly magical. Particularly, this is so, when the person viewing an aura does so for the first time.

My husband had never witnessed an aura before until one drizzly evening in Southern California. We were waiting (I sense a pattern here) for our turns to go back for our weekly massage. Inside the small anteroom, we sat together in low light listening to Japanese wood-chimes playing through speakers as a wall fountain trickled water—all intended to calm the rush of daily life outside. It worked. I immediately relaxed, as, apparently, did my husband.

My turn came first, and I went happily into the massage room with a masseuse I knew was a Native American shaman. Lucky me! The massage was marvelous, as always. I thanked her and, afterward, met my husband in the hallway. As we made our way to the front, my husband turned to me and scowled.

"What's with the blue light shining behind your masseuse? Why does this place do that to her?"

I started laughing (which he didn't appreciate). "Honey, there wasn't any blue light. That was her aura. *You* saw an *aura*!"

It took a while for him to understand just what that meant—even longer for him to believe it.

>< *big smile* ><

So, what exactly is an aura?

Historically, the explanation for an aura is *an electromagnetic field surrounding the human body*. Scientifically, auras are dismissed as a neurophysiologic phenomenon causing cross-wiring of the brain, also known as *synesthetes*. In either case, scientists agree that our bodies are made up of atoms, electrons, neutrons, protons, and the spaces between them. Their constant movement creates energy—the effects visible under certain photographic mechanisms, felt and utilized in modern medicine (think defibrillation of a heart), and seen by the naked eye as an aura.

SO, HOW DO I KNOW THIS IS REAL?

Traditionally, Japanese scientists and physicians ascribe to the practice of healing auras as a priority in treating physiologic disorders. This does not mean Japanese physicians fail to treat medical illnesses or trauma. Rather, they heal the aura in combination with physiological treatments. A focus on healing auras is a significant part of an individual's wellness plan and is paramount for many practicing healers of varied cultures.

For those who doubt the validity of auras, consider, for a moment, the image you see above hot asphalt on a summers' day. The heat radiates above the road, occasionally causing a mirage. This phenomenon has been experienced by nearly everyone.

Auras radiate in the same manner, only in color.

Now, take a look at your naked hand or foot. Be sure to use a pale, neutral-colored (ivory, grey, white, tan) blank wall as the backdrop for your observation. Now, just stare at your hand. Let your eyes soften. Wait.

Eventually, some may see a pale white light surrounding the exterior of the hand or foot. This may only be millimeters in size, but it's visible. Occasionally, you may notice a soft pale color rising from the white, and just like the heat waves from the road, it radiates upward, outward. For some, the light color may be large, even moving. For others, it remains tight against the skin, almost an outline of the hand or foot.

This is an aura.

Color is made up of energy—but not all colors have the same energy. The different wavelengths of color have different amounts of energy. For example, violet contains more energy than red. This energy (color) is part of what we experience, as "energy beings," ourselves. When we see auras, we are visualizing that person's, plant's, animal's, or object's energy.

An aura's color not only has different amounts of energy; the colors also reflect a different meaning. In addition, the colors can change within minutes. Our moods change almost as rapidly, so, why wouldn't our energy fields, as well? Typically, energy matches our internal self: emotions, physical health, thoughts, attitude, the chakras, etc. The auric field will display what's going on inside—a great clue for those seeking clarity.

Typical color meanings for auras are listed below (please note - this is not a comprehensive list):

- *Red* - passionate, dynamic, fearless
- *Pink* - gentle, loving, kind
- *Orange* - creativity, sensual, emotional
- *Yellow* - logical, analytical
- *Green* - unconditional love, healer, animal lover
- *Blue* - expressive, caring, nurturing, psychic
- *Indigo* - intuitive, deeply spiritual
- *Violet* - dynamic, charismatic, visionary
- *White** - purity, truth, transcendence

*It should be noted that nearly everyone has a small white aura that runs the peripheral edge of a person's body. This is not the same as a pure white aura—one that expands beyond the initial white 3+ mm outline seen on nearly everyone.

SO, WHAT'S THE BIG DEAL? WHY DOES THIS MATTER TO ME?

Visions aren't always that...a vision. At times, we all see things we question—shadows out of the corner of our eye, images of someone we know that has passed on, or colors surrounding a person's head or body.

These are real.

Energy, though we can't always see it, exists all around us, all of the time (think about radio waves). Occasionally, our ability to see these colors presents to us and we notice a person's aura. Again, it's real, and if it happens to you, consider yourself blessed!

SO, HOW DO I KNOW THIS IS REAL?

CHAPTER 4
Those Voices in My Head

"I HEARD ..."

Almost every spiritualist, psychic or medium has said this. How they actually "hear" is diverse, however. Clair-audience is the term used to describe a *hearing* event—something that spiritualists, psychics, and mediums alike utilize almost daily. The actual method with which each person receives clairaudience varies.

Interestingly, I've witnessed many non-psychics and non-medium individuals express the same: they "hear" things they cannot explain. I'm not talking about psychotic events that frequent mental health disorders. I'm talking about people with established mental clarity and psycho-social functionality that *hear* things they cannot explain.

These events don't make an individual "crazy" or invite a quick visit to a psychiatrist. Rather, these are events that signal the thinning of the veil between mortal life and those who have passed. These are real events, not crazy hallucinations of the mind.

Real sounds. Real voices. Real experiences.

My own clairaudience comes as voices that I hear—people who call out my name (I believe it is my grandfather, as this voice sounds exactly like my dad's voice, who is still very much alive and resides in another state, whereas, my grandfather passed 52 years ago). I have heard pounding or knocking when my attention was needed, as well. Needless-to-say, when this happens at night, I'm startled awake—something my husband doesn't appreciate, always. In addition, I often "hear" words or phrases, akin to "hearing" a song playing over and over in my head (some call that an "ear-worm").

These sounds are given as a means to understand and *hear* communication from the other side of the veil.

Nearly everyone has experienced that moment while driving a car when, suddenly, you hear, "Stop!" Instinctively, you hit the brakes and catch your breath as a wayward animal or rogue vehicle darts into your path. Had you not listened, you surely would have collided, to everyone's detriment. Those are called "close calls" by most of us. To some, that "close call" is actually a spiritual event. Identifying exactly who shouted "Stop!" is left unanswered. As a result, the acknowledgement of *hearing* the warning shout, "Stop!" is less frequently mentioned, though never forgotten.

Why is it that we are afraid to mention these types of experiences? Why are we so afraid to talk freely about the "voices" heard from unexplained sources?

My thought is that ridicule or an accusation of "hallucination" or the fear of being labeled "crazy" is to blame. Perhaps, a more open acceptance of these auditory messages (aka: voices in our minds) and the unexplained communications we hear would help us live happier, safer lives. Even as a warning, acknowledging these "admonitions" would help each of us to *listen to* more—pay better attention to these alerts and advisements.

So, how does someone know if this is real? How, exactly, do we know when a thought is just a thought and clairaudience is really happening?

The answer is: it's personal.

Each one of us receives information in different ways. We all receive, and we all respond. But how information is processed—how messages are perceived is as individual as each of our personalities. Many have talked of a sudden thought that pops into their head. Is this a written statement that is *read* in the mind or a voiced comment that is *heard*? These are only two possible ways of receiving information from a Higher Power. Perhaps the thought came from an image that suddenly flashed into mind. Again, this is a valid source of receiving the message from others in Spirit.

The challenge is to accept and then listen. Doubt about the manner in which information is received is the best way to turn-off any spiritual message. Allowing self-doubt to overtake the messages that are being given drowns out the information and stops the flow. Our job is to believe, receive, and record (or act) on the messages that we receive—not question the means from which we receive it. Audio thoughts, flashed images, "gut feelings," etc. are all impressions—messages from the Divine.

WHY SHOULD THIS MATTER TO ME? WHAT IF OTHERS THINK I'M CRAZY?

Truthfully, people think other people *are* crazy! It doesn't matter if you're choosing to skydive, swim with sharks, create artwork, write a book, develop new technology, or delve into holistic medical school. There will be those who call you "crazy" for trying new things, even "crazy" to follow your passion. Those naysayers are acting from a place of fear. Doubt colors their view of life, immobilizing their ability to take risks.

Listening to the inner voice that prompts and inspires us is very risky. It means we are willing to look beyond the explainable and open our minds to the possibility that there is a higher power with knowledge we've not yet discovered. This includes receiving information from a spiritual place.

Let me give you an example: 200 years ago, healers were burned as witches. Their medical practices weren't understood by the majority of the community they served. In the 19th century, washing hands before or after surgery (or delivering a baby) was considered ridiculous. People died because no one washed their hands. It was a lack of knowledge about infection and sterile procedure at the time. Those who touted sterility and hand-washing were considered crazy!

Consider this: a healer in the early 1800's receives inspired information to use electricity to "shock" a heart into beating properly. In that century, the healer would be considered no less than a Frankenstein mad-man, or worse, a witch. No doubt a mob would gather and take the healer to the nearest stake and set her afire—especially if her patient actually lived!

Fast forward to today. In my job as an emergency department RN, one of my duties is to use electricity to "shock" a heart into a normal rhythm. This procedure is called "defibrillation" and is part of my job. Refusing to do so could result in disciplinary action and/or discharge from my place of employment. Never have I worried that "shocking a heart" back to its normal rhythm would result in my being labeled a "mad-man" and dragged into the parking lot to be burned at the stake.

So, what is the difference between the two scenarios?

Information. Someone had to discover that electricity would defibrillate a failing heart. That information was definitely inspired. Time caught up with the acceptance of that information and the process of defibrillation is now protocol in every hospital's "Code Blue"—still saving lives (and to my knowledge, nurses aren't burned at the stake in the parking lot for defibrillating a patient, either).

This is important to understand because the messages you receive come from Spirit—just as the knowledge to defibrillate a heart came from a Higher Source. You may be receiving information now that is considered advanced and will be readily accepted as "the norm" a few centuries in the future. In fact, receiving thoughts audibly may be the means to communicate and receive vital information in just a few short decades.

Don't be afraid to be ahead of the game!
Don't be afraid to listen.

CHAPTER 5
Stop Touching Me!

My kids used to say that all of the time—especially on road trips. It made me nuts! There was no possible way for us to travel in the car, even ten minutes, without someone touching his neighbor. The kids just couldn't keep their hands to themselves!

Believe it or not, it's the same with those on the other side of the veil. Some of those souls cannot keep their touchy-feely hands to themselves either. People talk with their hands; we take the arm of someone we want to listen to us; a gentle touch for emphasis, etc. The same is true with spirits. They "reach out" to us, trying to get our attention, hoping we'll notice.

Perhaps we unknowingly noticed.

We've all experienced it—that sudden chill that runs the length of our spine, a soft brush of ethereal fingers running through our hair, the unexpected encounter with an unseen hand on our arm or shoulder. You know the feeling. Perhaps it's a sensation that someone has just taken the vacant seat next to you or planted themselves on the edge of your bed (you feel the mattress suddenly compress but when you look, nothing is there).

Yes, admit it...we've all experienced it.

These subtle reminders that the veil is incredibly thin and souls on the other side are literally reaching out to us can be unsettling. This is the stuff of horror films and psychological thrillers. That unsolicited touch makes us jump...and not always for joy.

But it doesn't have to be that way.

Almost without exception, the living will experience an occurrence called a "tell" that happens when spiritual events are about to take place. For me, it's a tingling in my scalp or and itchy palm (often it's my nose that itches). These *tells* help alert us to phenomenon that is under way (or about to take place) from the other side.

We all have experienced chills down our spine or goosebumps on our skin (I'm talking about the times this happens when the temperature is cozy—not cold). These unexpected physical responses are reactions to perceived occurrences. Even when we cannot visualize exactly what's happening, our body lets us know something is going on. Our subsequent reaction is to interpret the sensation—give it meaning. Often, we react that this is uncomfortable, which comes about from a lifetime of conditioning. We're trained to believe that these feelings mean "bad" (ie: goosebumps or chills often make us feel "uncomfortable" as a result).

I believe these reactions were once perceived as neither "good" or "bad," they just happened without analysis. This likely took place when we were very young, inexperienced with the norms of "real life," and open to receiving whatever messages came from a spiritual plane—all without judgment. Perhaps that is the way we are meant to receive these *tells*. Perhaps we are simply meant to receive in a non-judgmental manner. Think what would happen then?

Consider what would take place if we were to reframe our perception of these physiological reactions? Imagine receiving a *tell* without judgment.

Think about a time when you heard good news that was so surprising, it gave you goosebumps. If you cannot think of a time, pretend you just won the jackpot on a slot machine. Wouldn't that be a positive experience your body would alert you to (ie: rapid heart rate, flushed cheeks, the urge to shout for joy, etc.)? Now, think about the last time you heard news that made you literally cry "tears of joy." The physical response that produces these kinds of tears often happens when a baby is born.

Physiological reaction to a perceived mental stimulus is real. It happens constantly. Our greatest challenge is to *listen* and remain *non-judgmental* about what we receive and how we respond.

To listen on a spiritual level, it isn't necessary to hear sounds audibly, as discussed in the previous chapter. Spiritual messages are often described as "a whisper." Hearing in spirit happens simply by paying attention. A *knowing* takes place that validates you've heard the message being sent. Physical reactions substantiate, as well as alert us (aka: via *tells*). Most of us appreciate validation—whether for accomplishment, ideas, or spiritual insight. Validation helps us feel certain that our assumptions are correct. It's a safety thing. When something validates our thoughts or actions, we can relax and know we're on the right path.

The same is true for validations of spiritual thoughts or impressions. Goosebumps, chills, itchy noses (although somewhat irritating) are forms of validation that something's about to happen and our intuitive sense is true. Remaining non-judgmental, even when our previous habit includes categorizing an event as "good" or "bad," is key to spotting more easily the *tells* as they come. It's like noticing a certain number, for example 11:11 on a clock, and then seeing it many times throughout the day—on a street sign, on a bill, etc. When you start to notice and accept the signs (*tells*) and subsequent information (message), you begin to notice their occurrence more often.

These are literally memorandums to guide you through life.

TELL YOUR *TELLS*

So, what are the most common *tells* and how do I recognize mine?

It's a lot like the irises in our eyes. The color of human eyes falls into a few basic categories: blue, brown, green, and hazel. Of course, there are more, but let's use those four for our example.

Occasionally, people are classified by their eye color. Traits are assigned to an eye color. Heritage is recognized by eye color. And so on and so on and so on...

Did you know that our irises are another "fingerprint" for our body? We each have a unique iris pattern and color scheme that does not match anyone else. If you look closely at another person's iris, you will see color, flecks, rings, and patterns. The general color may be the same in two people, but the patterns and color arrangement is unique.

So, *why* talk about the uniqueness of the human iris?

Because the uniqueness of an iris is similar to a psychic *Clair*. Just like your iris, that has color, flecks, and patterns (multiple factors that make up your individual iris), YOU have multiple psychic *clairs* that make up your spiritual gifts. Accompanying those are specific *tells* (the forewarning that a psychic gift has been keyed up and will come through momentarily).

We'll get into the *clairs* later on. For now, let's look at the *tells* a little deeper.

TELLS WILL TELL US—THE SPIRITUAL PHONE IS RINGING

These precursory warnings signal that a spiritual message (or "download") is about to happen—and come through when least expected. Perhaps that is the reason spiritual *tells* exist in the first place. Usually, we go about our business without thinking of messages from the spirit world. It's as if we've turned our spiritual phone to silent and set it down.

Something has to get our attention when a message is en route.

Tells are that message. A *tell* is the otherworldly phone ringing from a divine caller that snaps our focus from things of this realm to things of a spiritual nature. Within moments, the *clairs* are activated and we receive information.

Below is a list of a few common *tells*:

SO, HOW DO I KNOW THIS IS REAL?

- Ringing in the ears
- Itchy or tingling palms
- Chills down arms, legs or back
- Tingling scalp or neck
- Blurred vision
- Dizziness

Many other *tells* could easily make the list. These are unique and individual. Your *tell* may be different from anyone else and not found on the list above. That doesn't mean it's not a *tell*. It just means that particular *tell* belongs to you! In fact, you may have multiple *tells* that alert you to a specific *clair* coming through, letting you know that you're about to receive inspiration.

You will know.

I NEVER GET ANY OF THIS. SO, WHY DOES THIS MATTER TO ME?

Doubt and skepticism are the enemies of spirituality. Most religions call this the absence of faith. We're all taught to question everything—a good position to take, unless it is used to the extreme. Truth can be discovered with appropriate questioning, but when that truth reveals itself to be something a little unexpected, we naturally begin to doubt and turn away. We'll talk a little more about expectations and how those are deal-breakers in spiritual communication.

Recognizing and utilizing our personal *tells* allows us to drop the skepticism, move away from doubt, and live in faith. When we receive our *tell*, we can know with certainty that the message we will inevitably receive is of a spiritual nature. The trick is to recognize the *tell* and then assign it to the appropriate symbol or message. Doing this on a consistent basis allows us to live a life filled with faith, compassion, and peace.

Choosing to live a life receiving and responding to the *tells* that come to us brings security. Making this a daily part of life brings peace. Knowing the *tell* serves us is an important and loving way to live.

CHAPTER 6
Clarify the Clair!

CLAIRVOYANCE IS THE ALLEGED ABILITY to gain information about an object, person, location, or physical event through extrasensory perception. Any person who is claimed to have such ability is said accordingly to be a clairvoyant. (Wikipedia)

How many times have you driven your car, listened to music, and enjoyed beautiful blue skies that filter golden sunlight, warming your soul? The day couldn't be better. You feel grounded and at peace.

Suddenly, you hear, "Stop!"

On impulse, your muscles clench and you slam your foot on the brake just in time to miss a wayward vehicle that darts unaware into your path. You have no idea where the voice came from or who shouted at you, but you know it was real...and likely saved your life.

We've all experienced something like this: a warning voice, the familiar scent of a deceased loved one's perfume, the unexplained sense that someone is about to call just before the phone rings (and we know exactly who it is).

I could go on and on and on...

These occurrences are not accidental. Nor are they to be ignored. These incidences are spiritual and recognized by one of many different *clairs*.

Everyone has at least one *clair* (whether he wants to admit it or not) and many people have multiple *clairs*. The trick is to recognize, accept, and receive the message that is coming through when one of the *clairs* is activated. In the situation with the car (described above), typically the driver doesn't have time to question the source or reality of the voice's message—instead, he recognizes the urgency and reacts instinctively. This is a powerful *clair* that leaps over rationale to help our instincts to react.

Most messages come with a *tell*, and an accompanying shadow of doubt. Even though our skin crawls or our ears suddenly buzz, it's as if a non-tangible message isn't real to our logical brain. We doubt, dismiss, and pay the consequences later on.

Almost without exception, when we receive a *tell*, it precedes the warning that a specific *clair* is about to open up. Too often, we ignore the *tell*. Still, the message arrives. When we choose to ignore and dismiss the *tell*, we are essentially hanging up on our spiritual phone call—rejecting the message in the process.

How does that work for anyone?

So, let's choose to not ignore our *tells* and, ultimately, the *clairs* that follow. The messages will be profound, and the practice will likewise become a part of life, ultimately changing our course for the better. In addition, as each of us accept and recognize the activation of our *clair(s)*, we will become stronger in the use of them. In other words, doubt will abandon us, and we will be left with certainty.

How wonderful would it be to know that the inspiration you receive is from a spiritual realm, always? How comforting to know that God speaks to us directly—answering questions, guiding, providing, directing us all!

WHAT ARE THE *CLAIRS*, EXACTLY?

Let's talk about these *clairs*. Let's discuss specifically what they are so that we can recognize *clairs* as they inspire us daily. Spiritualist have identified from six to more than a dozen *clairs*. Below, I have listed seven of the most common. The nature of the *clair* is in parentheses (what it does). Examples of what that *clair* does is listed, as well.

Take a look at the list below and make note (in the margins or on a separate piece of paper) of all of the *clairs* you have experienced:

SO, HOW DO I KNOW THIS IS REAL?

- **Clair voyance** – (SEE)
    - images
    - ghosts
    - scry
    - ruins
    - aura
    - synchronicities
    - patterns
    - cards
    - tea leaves
    - etc.

- **Clair sentience** – (FEEL)
    - empath
    - (aura)
    - objects (crystals, houses, artifacts, nature)
    - investigations in hauntings

- **Clair tangency** – (TOUCH)
    - objects
    - psychometry

- **Clair audience** – (HEAR)
    - voices
    - messages in head/mind (like a song or reading to self)
    - audible (name called out, pounding on wall)

- **Clair cognizance** – (KNOWING)
    - "gut feeling"
    - "just know" environmental, people, situational

- **Clair alience** – (SMELL)
    - scents associated with loved ones (Jergins & Clorox)
    - smoke
    - decay

- **Clair gustance** – (TASTE)
    - metallic
    - food
    - blood
    - vomit

There are many more *clairs* not listed above. If you feel that you have been given a *clair* not on this list, please include that *clair* in your personal list. Remember, *these* are as individual as our fingerprints (or the patterns and colors of our irises)—a special, unique gift meant for each of us, individually.

Once you have your list, pay attention to your thoughts and feelings whenever one of these *clairs* are activated. You might consider keeping a journal of *clair* experiences and the message that accompanies it.

Again, for many, a *tell* precedes the *clair*, alerting us to "pay attention." Below is a list of common *tells*. Take a look at these and write them down next to the *clair* you experience. Think about the *tell* and note if it accompanies more than one *clair*. Compare the *clairs* to see if there is a similarity between them (ie: claircognizance and clairsentience – commonly seen in empaths).

If you are having a difficult time recognizing your *tell(s)*, ask yourself the question: "What happens first?" and "How do I know?" Look for a physical reaction just prior to the advent of the *clair*.

HOW DO I KNOW?

Psychic *TELLS*:

- chills
- leg aches
- itch
- buzzing in ears
- dizziness
- dreams
- physical illnesses or pain
- dreams
- patterns (11:11)
- compelled (to do something)

The next step is to look for a pattern:

- What *clair(s)* have I experienced?

- What happened just before I experience this *clair*?

- What is the message?

SO, HOW DO I KNOW THIS IS REAL?

Look for similarities in the messages, the *clair* used to deliver the message, and the *tell* alerting you to the *clair's* activation. Once you have been able to list these in a manner that seems organized and consistent, it's time to ask the most important question:

Why?

CHAPTER 7
That Spiritual Telephone Won't Stop Ringing

Exactly why someone receives spiritual messages (and why, it seems, others do not) is a personal issue. My opinion is that everyone receives messages but not everyone recognizes or accepts them. The responsibility falls to each individual.

It's like answering a phone call, only the call is placed from a spiritual source. Whether we pay attention to the incessant ringing that begs for our attention and answer the call makes all the difference. In everyday life, we may opt to ignore a phone call and let the party on the other end hang up after a time (most likely, the caller is frustrated and just gives up on trying to reach us).

What if that is exactly how our Higher Source works?

In truth, our spiritual calls come more frequently than we often recognize. Whether we hear the spiritual "ring" depends on how in-tune we are. Some may not even recognize that the "ring" is just that—a signal to answer a spiritual call and receive an intuitive message.

Once we identify what our spiritual telephone's ringtone sounds like, we can be attuned to its frequency and literally listen for it. Our job, so to speak, is to pay attention and when that ringer goes off, decide whether we will answer the call or not. The Divine calls frequently, fortunately, but does not pester us, unfortunately. If we choose not to heed the call and decide we don't want to answer, God calls less frequently. The call may even go to someone else.

More likely, we don't remember what the Divine's ring tone sounds like and we fail to answer.

Fortunately, for those who have forgotten what a spiritual ring tone (aka: "*tell*") sounds like, a quick reminder and lots of attention will bring us back on task. This reminder allows us to recognize and answer the call.

That's great news!

Too often, our brains shift into high-gear, threatening to raise the thought-decibels to a point that we cannot hear the Divine. People who struggle with meditation call this occurrence, "busy minds." It's not uncommon and is, actually, a wonderful gift (creative people have exceptionally busy brains). Learning to manage the activity, quality, and direction of thought is key. Again, it's all about recognition of the *tell*. The interruption of thought that is different and signals the specific ringtone for a spiritual call is what we're listening for. Discovery of that process is tricky sometimes.

Meditation is the way.

SO, HOW DO I KNOW?

I chose the title of this book for a reason. Many of my clients have asked this question. How do I really know I'm receiving inspiration or spiritual messages?

This answer is this: You are!

Just know that you *do* receive messages from a higher spiritual source, from the Divine, from God. The catch is, are you paying attention to those? Do you stop and listen, and then not doubt?

Most of us wallow in self-doubt and question any thought or possible intuitive idea that comes to mind. This is common, and the one habit that kills spiritual recognition. Let me give you a quick list of tasks that you can do to *receive* and *recognize* spiritual insight (and by the way, this list came to me via my own inspirational, spiritual "phone call").

SO, HOW DO I KNOW THIS IS REAL?

The MESSAGE of this discussion is to:
1) Pay attention
2) Stop doubting or questioning
3) Release all judgment when thoughts do arise
4) Redirect thoughts into your intention
5) Receive whatever comes into mind
6) Record (make a list of your *tells* so you'll know for the future)
7) Meditate—the tool

Remember when we talked about becoming the spiritual "tool" for inspiration? There are three steps to doing this:

Receive—Record—Release

When you receive insight (or what you sense is a spiritual message or inspiration), go through the numbered list above:

1) Stop what you are doing (as much as is possible). I've often been forced to pull my car to the side of the road in order to receive a message, undistracted from traffic and the process of driving (something those sharing the road with me probably appreciate). The physical process of stopping signals to your spiritual source that you are ready to listen and receive. Stopping takes the form of mentally ceasing your busy mind's activity. By closing your eyes (if that helps) and moving into silence physically (stop making "noise" with your body) and emotionally, and then notice the breath, you signal that you are actively listening.

2) Once you've received the message, record your impressions. Remember, the message can come as an intuitive thought, different from "busy brain" chatter. These spiritual messages come as impressions or *knowing*, images, sounds, smells, feeling, etc. (think of the *clairs* we discussed in the previous chapter). Accept the message from your spiritual source. Even if it seems a little

crazy or makes no sense, just accept it as a message. You do not have to judge or interpret the message. At this point in the process, you only receive.

3) Record the message as best you can. Some people opt to journal their spiritual impressions, others choose to draw the inspiration received. Using adjectives to describe (versus nouns that label an impression) will give a broader foundation to recognize what that message is. This is the tool that Remote Viewers use, and its accuracy has been proven scientifically.

4) I cannot impress upon you the importance of recording your thoughts and impressions. Dream journals and psychotherapy diaries have illuminated the benefits of journaling. In addition, doing so frees the recipient from holding onto a specific thought, allowing him (or her) to receive more. It also frees us from the need to interpret the message—that can be done later, when needed.

5) Last but not least in importance is the powerful tool of meditation. Allowing your spirit and body to go to stillness is one of the most formidable gifts you can give to yourself. By meditating, we allow our spirit to "digest" the information we've received while opening ourselves up to receive more. It's a practice that deepens our ability to recognize and receive spiritual gifts.

6) I believe meditation is the forgotten side of prayer. Jesus Christ taught man to "*Be still* and *know* that I am..." (italics added). His teachings about stillness and knowing is found in holy scripture. In the Christian tradition, when we pray, we often thank God for our blessings and ask Him to bless others, then we close in His name with an "Amen."

We forget to listen. We forget to "be still and know," as Jesus taught us.

SO, HOW DO I KNOW THIS IS REAL?

I believe the "stillness" Jesus refers to is meditation. It's exactly what Jesus asks us to do in prayer...in life. It's also exactly what Buddhists practice to on their path to enlightenment.

During prayer, after we've expressed thanks and asked for the blessing of others, if we sit in silence and *listen*, our souls go to stillness. In those moments of stillness, we receive inspiration—direct messages from God. It is as if the Divine is speaking directly to us. We're on a spiritual phone call with our Higher Source. Let's not make this a one-sided conversation by doing all the talking during the call then hanging up ("Amen"). Let's go to stillness and just listen to what God has to tell us.

Meditation is a vital tool for accomplishing this.

THIS IS ALL SO TECHNICAL AND, REALLY, TMI! WHY DO I HAVE TO KNOW ALL OF THIS STUFF? WHY CAN'T I JUST LET IT HAPPEN AND NOT IDENTIFY IT?

Well, actually, you can. You can just "let go and let God," and hope that you recognize what's happening to you when it does. Or, you can identify your *clairs* and notice the tells that precede them, making yourself available and prepared to answer the spiritual call that will come.

The choice is yours. How you decide to handle your inspiration and the messages from the Divine is entirely up to you.

CHAPTER 8
Conversations with the Dead

THIS IS A CHAPTER THAT probably isn't meant for everyone. I know there are those of you who have no interest in conversing with the dead.

I was one of those. I had no interest in interacting with the deceased...once.

The shift (from fear of ghosts, to curiosity about spirits, to the desire to connect with souls who have crossed over) happened slowly. In fact, one of my mentors brought it up.

"Have you seen people walking around who don't know they're dead yet?" she casually asked one day.

"What!" My response included a gasp somewhere.

"Uh-huh. Okay, then. Get ready, 'cause it's going to happen soon." I could hear the smile in her voice and decided to keep her phone number on speed dial just in case she was right.

That conversation gave birth to the horrifying thought that maybe I was destined to really see ghosts. I envisioned that famous movie about the little boy who saw dead people, "...all the time."

No thanks! Not me. Nope!

Well, time has changed a few things, mainly my perspective. With added experience, time deepened my understanding about what it means to communicate with those who have passed. Again, a shift from fear to understanding. Isn't that how these things usually work?

My cathartic moment came during a walking meditation with my dog. It was unplanned. Normally, my playlist includes Aerosmith and

Zeppelin but that day I felt prompted to "tune in" to Tibetan singing bowls and just "listen."

I'm so glad that I did.

Within moments of just walking, breathing, absorbing the sounds of the bowls, and calming my ever-busy brain, I noticed the trees. Sentinels, really. I could *feel* their spirits—sense the immense safety and peace in their life source. These are living, breathing, energetic spiritual entities that share our planet and watch over us. Their calling is divine.

I immediately felt at one with these magnificent trees and realized that my spirit shares the same space as theirs. I could literally *feel* that space. We've all heard this before. But for some reason, in this moment, the concept was powerful and touched my soul. I realized, also, that when I lack the ability to *feel* their spirits, I only have myself to blame. The distractions in my life get in the way of connecting with their energy—not the other way around. It's all on me.

It was in this moment that I realized the souls who have crossed over also share this space. They are no different than the trees. The lack of communication with them falls on me! I suddenly understood how to connect with spirits who have passed on.

So how do we do it?

The answer came almost immediately upon asking: "You connect with them the same way you connect with the trees. You go to that spiritual stillness that is not distracted, that *feels,* that communicates on all levels—with the living and the dead."

Spiritual eyes are the answer and they can only be opened when in the "spiritual zone." So, where does one find this zone, you may ask. The answer comes in a definition of mind versus brain that I learned when I first started down my spirituality pathway. In a nutshell, it is this:

> **Brain** consists of physical grey matter, vessels, fluid, electrical impulses, and cells encased within cranial bones in the body. Brain allows the functions of the body to take

SO, HOW DO I KNOW THIS IS REAL?

place. Brain also provides the mechanism for analytical thought, calculations, rationalization, protocol and task mechanics, and other thought-processes.

Mind is less definitive, yet equal in function. Within the Mind, one stores memories, emotions, wisdom, personal experience, spiritual understanding, among other experiential history. Mind is where we find stillness. This is the place that we reach Source. Mind is where we connect with all things spiritual.

To separate this into complete finite functions is unrealistic. Mind and Brain blend to create our experience and knowledge. However, understanding that each has a separate function while working together, allows us to tap into both physical and spiritual.

Let me give you an example of this on the physical plane in hopes of clarifying this truth. Think of your lower extremities. Just as the right foot and left foot are separate, both work in tandem to help create the body's gait. The Brain and Mind work in the same independent manner, unified in purpose. One cannot have an experience without some form of knowledge about that experience. At the same time, knowledge occurs when we experience life. These cannot be separated.

Depending on the situation, you may choose to use Brain function (ie: CPR is not likely effective with only prayers of "white light" and "healing energy." I'm not saying those things couldn't work, but history dictates that algorithms and protocols learned through specialized training, practice, and memory allow us to perform this life-saving intervention properly). Working meticulously through a memorized protocol allows one to perform life-saving measures in this situation. This is learned knowledge. This is the Brain at work.

Tapping into the Divine, on the other hand, is not something you can follow an algorithm to perform. The process requires the conscious effort of "letting go" of thought and judgment and reaching deep into the soul with Mind attentiveness. As we reach that spiritual place, we experience stillness and spiritual intuition. This is Mind at work.

In case you're entirely confused by the above, let me try to put this into a simplistic "how-to" description (wish me luck!):

To reach spiritual heights and connect with our Higher Selves, we need to go deep into our inner being—into our soul. This is accomplished through stillness. I'm not talking about not moving (although that helps some people), I'm talking about calming our Brain, quieting our thoughts, and moving into a state that notices our many senses. This is living in the moment.

Meditation is the process. The breath is the tool.

There is no special trick or shortcut to get to this state. One must practice going into stillness. Like Yoga, it takes time to get your body, brain and mind to strike the position that holds you in your stillness. Once you feel comfortable getting to that state, you can begin to tap into your senses.

Notice whatever your mind "hears" (clairaudience), whatever you sense (clairsentience), whatever your mouth tastes (clairgustance), whatever your nose smells (clairsalience), whatever your closed eyes "see" (clairvoyance), and whatever your knowing tells you from deep within (claircongizance). Call upon your *clairs* to assist you with recognizing the messages from spiritual sources.

Those who have passed dwell in this realm. Souls who no longer live in physical bodies speak in this language. Our job is to recognize and receive them. Listen to what they have to say. Feel their spiritual messages. Record our experience with them. Never judge.

This is the language of the Higher Self.

It is here that you will speak, feel and, possibly, see those who have crossed.

SO, HOW DO I KNOW THIS IS REAL?

WHAT IF I'M AFRAID TO SEE DEAD PEOPLE? WHY WOULD I WANT TO EVEN KNOW HOW TO DO THAT?

You never have to experience anything from the spiritual realm that you don't want to. Know this!

You always have the option to state (out loud is best) that you do not wish to communicate with anyone who has passed on. Send that intention out, ask that you will not be privy to connect with the other side, and then relax. It won't happen.

For those who wish to enhance or initiate contact with the "other side," the tools are listed above. It requires patience, practice, and persistent openness to the messages as they come.

CHAPTER 9
What Do They Really Think?

I HAVE A NAGGING THOUGHT—AN image that literally makes my stomach wrench and my pores sweat, overtime! It begins with, "What if...?"

...My grandparents and aunt, along with a few friends, and some other relatives are standing on the other side of "the veil" (aka: they are all dead) and staring at me?

I imagine them with their arms are folded, looking down from a big open space, expressionless. I can't tell exactly what they are thinking. For some reason, it feels incredibly important for me to know their opinion of me and my spirituality. I want to know if they approve (and if they disapprove). Their impression of me and my work matters.

This seems crazy because a "calling" to live in spirituality is much bigger than people's opinion, including those who have passed. Still, the angst doesn't dissipate when I give myself that self-reprimand to "Let it go" and stop the unwarranted worry.

It simply doesn't go away.

Because this just happened again yesterday. I had accidently connected with someone from the other side. The situation related to a tragedy that I was unaware of at the time (very emotional). My need for approval filtered through my connection and shifted my focus away from the message.

It was disappointing, at best.

Resultingly, I feel the need to stop and discuss how to handle family and friends, associates, co-workers...whoever rejects or mocks someone who uses spiritual gifts. The urge to "let go" surfaces again, paramount to staying "in-tune" with the Spirit. It made me realize this truth once again.

Spirituality and its associated gifts can be both a blessing and a curse.

The blessing part seems obvious: we stay close to our higher power, live with intent, manifest our needs and desires, communicate with loved ones crossed over, and serve those who seek us. It seems that should be enough, right?

The "curse" part is what makes this a challenge. Family and friends, who have known you from the time of your birth (or so it seems) remember the part of you that did not include your spiritual gifts. Those who "came into" their spiritual gifts later in life, perhaps after a life-changing event, keenly feel the projected doubt of others. A few have lived an entire lifetime on this earth honoring and practicing the skills and spiritual gifts they were born with. For a few, family, friends, and associates accepted you in wholeness—including your gifts. To those who fit this latter description, I have tremendous respect (and feel a little envious) for you.

Of course, this assumes you've been recognized as a Spiritualist. It also assumes you honor yourself as such, as well.

For the rest, the process of earning respect and acknowledgement is a little more difficult. Our associates and loved ones may not take the same receptive attitude. Knowing the nuances of an individual's personality *before* the spirituality became public knowledge can be a hinderance toward acceptance.

Family and friends will often shake a doubtful head and move away. This can be an actual distancing that happens on an emotional plane—very painful, indeed.

Unfortunately, I have no solution, except to be patient and show love in return. It is my belief that when someone demonstrates love in response to negativity, those loving actions speak the loudest. With time, people realize their misconception about spiritualists and recognize the love behind the intent in spiritual work, mediumship, energy healings, etc. Many naysayers come around, in time, to support their gifted loved one. Of course, this doesn't hold true for everyone, but for those individuals who experience the love and acceptance of family and friends (those who support the spiritually gifted), the reward is magnificent!

Always remember that, as a spiritualist, you cannot force another individual to understand or believe in you. The acceptance process takes time and can be lengthy—perhaps never to take place. Your job is to demonstrate your intent. Be loving. Be patient. Have faith in who you are and the spiritual gifts you possess.

By doing this, you allow your higher power to guide those who do not yet believe in you. This guidance takes them to the path of acceptance. That in itself can be miraculous and tremendous validation.

Love. Let God do the rest.

So how does someone coming into their spiritual gifts handle the angst that follows those that don't believe? I'm not sure there is a "pat answer" to that question. My experience with this belongs to me. I'll share my thoughts in hopes that some of you can relate and use "the error of my ways" to tread an easier path.

Again, love is the best answer. Silence is too.

"Sometimes, the silence speaks the loudest," said a very wise friend many years ago. I agree. When we allow the other person to speak, without interruption and without argument, a miraculous thing happens. When we allow the silence to be our voice, the speaker "hears" his own intent, and realizes the words he spoke does not match that intent. In other words, sometimes hearing oneself speak reveals the fallacy of the comments made. The trick is to allow the speaker the opportunity to hear himself without interruption.

Silence.

Arguments of a spiritual nature never work out. Filling the space between you and the naysayer with love and silence, does. Of course, I am not advocating for the allowance of verbal abuse—far from it.

My point is that we often jump into an argument before comments have had time to settle. This is a trap, usually, designed to produce dissention and discussion leading to bad feelings. Someone must win and someone must lose in these scenarios.

But what if a third option—a win-win option—is available? What if there is no argument but rather an "aha" moment of new understanding? The words must land, meaning must be digested, and understanding bubble up from the surface. That happens when speaking ceases.

And then...silence.

I believe our power comes in the silent *knowing* that truth *always* comes forward. If we speak our truth, we have nothing to worry about. The act of acceptance belongs to the person who chooses to doubt— it just takes that person a little longer to get there. Our responsibility is to recognize and hold fast to truth—even when it is challenged because it looks different than another's truth.

Fortunately, we don't have to referee truth—God does that. We don't have to decide when or how truth will surface—our higher power will do that for us at exactly the right time. Thankfully, we don't have to prove truth either—that's all on the Divine.

So, silence becomes our ally.

An ancient marshal art originating in Japan, Aikido, bases its philosophy on a win-win approach to combat. Sounds a little contradictory, doesn't it? This philosophy is based on the concept that neither party is injured. Someone attacks and the other person must act: defensively, with returned aggression, or with the intent to allow both parties to emerge unscathed. This happens when the recipient guides the energy between them.

In other words, a punch is thrown. The target of that punch guides the clenched fist aside so that the energy behind the punch doesn't cause injury to himself or the attacker. This is accomplished by guiding that fist away from the target. Typically, the energy expended by the attacker is diffused into thin air as the punch lands on nothing and

SO, HOW DO I KNOW THIS IS REAL?

the attacker stumbles forward. The target has stepped aside, allowing the attacker's energy to dissipate, while allowing himself to remain unharmed. Both attacker and target remain uninjured. Win-win.

I believe in the Aikido philosophy of life. With a little creativity, it's possible to face emotional conflict with a win-win outcome. Let me share an example of what I mean by this.

The phone rings (this call isn't from Spirit). Someone you know calls you up, then proceeds to verbally attack you by calling you names or swearing at you over the phone. You (the target) have two options: return the verbal assault by shouting back even more offensive insults (attack in return) or hang up (defend). So, what is the third option—the one that is the win-win? How does the Aikido philosophy option apply here?

Set the phone down on the counter and walk away. Don't announce your intent (attack) but rather, just quietly set the phone down. This allows the caller (attacker) to expel her energy without harming herself or you in the process. As soon as the caller wears out and loses interest in her rant, and she's released all of the energy she can muster, she stops. Likely too, she soon as she realizes her verbal punches are hitting empty air. There is no one to engage. The fight is over. She'll eventually hang up and you can too.

This exposes truth—you will not engage in defensive or attacking verbal combat. You honor yourself and the other person's opinion without accepting injury for either. Your truth is win-win. This is acting in a loving manner (toward yourself and the other person, even though you may not feel it at the time).

Remember to hold onto truth. Remember the knowledge of what our gifts include, how we use them, and how our intent brings power into stressful situations. Our ability to peaceably interact with those who would challenge us lies in our power. Love is the result—love for self and love for the other.

Love and Silence.

These are formidable tools to keep close at hand.

WHY DOES THIS MATTER TO ME? I LIKE A GOOD CHALLENGE! BRING IT ON, I SAY.

Well, the most important part of this whole discussion is spiritual in nature. Remember, contention and stress are the best repellants of spirituality. If you truly want to work as a light-worker, a spiritualist, be filled with positive energy, and help others—you can't do that in a fight.

Granted, there will be times when we all have to saddle up, hoist the colors, and draw the sword for a cause, but that should be rare and guided by our higher power—not out of spite. In fact, unless your name is Joan of Arc or Saint-Anything, I'd suggest a very prayerful approach to everything contentious. If, in the moment, you cannot pray about it and receive inspiration from God or your intuition, I'd suggest using my favorite go-to response: "Let me think about that and I'll get back with you." Then, get to stillness and find the answer. It works every time!

Bottom line—you can choose to live spiritually, peacefully, or you can choose to argue. You cannot choose both (most times). You also drive away spiritual messages when conflict becomes your companion. Of course, the choice is yours.

I'd suggest you choose the Aikido approach of peace, love and silence.

CHAPTER 10
Spirit Doesn't Speak English!

At this point in the book, some readers may notice this chapter's title and already be shaking their heads, muttering, "Well, duh!" Others may have just felt that flush of panic that accompanies the thought, *Yeah, well how do I know what Spirit's saying then?*

Great question!

Let me begin by stating that Spirit doesn't speak Swahili, Chinese, Hebrew or Latin either. If a specific language belonging to a specific culture was the modus operandi for communication with higher beings, we'd all be in trouble.

The opportunity to converse with the Holy Ones and receive the spiritual messages (received by those who listen) cannot belong to only one language or culture or locality. Spiritual conversation belongs to everyone everywhere. It doesn't matter what language that region of their world speaks. Spirit knows how to get around that geographical dilemma.

Because the Divine doesn't speak to us linguistically, our ability to understand and communicate with Spirit must come through a means less finite than human language. So, then, how does Spirit speak to us?

Symbols.

Spiritual language is the language of symbols. Our task is to recognize them. Be aware, each individual's symbolic language with the Divine is just as distinct as the person receiving it. No two receivers will recognize the same symbols as having identical meanings. In other words, your symbol for "love" may be a heart shape, while your favorite intuitive's symbol for that same meaning (love) may be the rose. Both are appropriate and easily recognized as symbols for the same meaning: love. So, neither of you are right, nor are either of you wrong. You just have a different symbol for love.

The same holds true in Asian printed languages. The Chinese symbol for love is "Ai" or 爱. The Korean symbol for the same is "salang" or 사랑. Both symbols have the same meaning, expressed in different modalities. Neither is good, bad, right, or wrong—they just have meaning assigned to them, the same way the heart and rose have meaning. The difference lies in how the meaning is interpreted and by whom.

Think of something very symbolic to you. Typically, symbolism is found around traditions or rituals. Let's use Valentine's Day as our example. Using imagery, once again, consider what symbol expresses the meaning behind Valentine's Day to you. When I mention this holiday, do you see cupid? Hearts? Chocolates? Flowers? A candle-lit dinner with someone? Sex?

Whatever you envisioned when Valentine's Day is mentioned—that is your symbol for February 14th. This is exactly how spiritual symbols work.

This is key to understanding how to "speak" spiritually.

As we discover the language of our Higher Power, we discover the symbols that soon have meaning to them (like the one you envisioned for Valentine's Day). A pattern emerges and the language of Spirit reveals itself. This pattern is sometimes difficult to see but once you pay attention and take note of these symbols (and their associated meanings), you'll have a list of "words" used by the Holy Ones to communicate to you.

So how does someone recognize a symbol?

Think back to our discussion in Chapter 6 about recognizing *tells* and their meanings? *Tells*, as you remember, are the "alerts" that comes to a person when he or she is about to receive a message. You may feel tingling down your spine as a friend describes a job interview. In your mind's eye, you see the flash of a dollar bill and/or a large bouquet of flowers.

The tingling is your *tell*. The image is your symbol.

As you recognize a *tell* when it presents, and then learn to pay attention to what happens next, you'll identify symbols that will have a pattern of meaning. Perhaps the image of a bouquet of flowers means "gift" to you. Perhaps the dollar bill means "money coming in" to you. When you take these two symbols together, you could interpret your friend's description of her job interview as having a very positive outcome! The job is a "gift" that will "bring in money" to her. The Divine has given you a message about that situation. Using your very unique spiritual language, you are able to receive and understand that happy message.

Consider this: you are watching football on the television, enjoying a nice evening at home. Suddenly, you hear ringing in your ears. Next, you smell peppermint, the kind Grandpa Jake used to keep tucked in a pocket. In your mind's eye, you might even see a flash of Grandpa Jake's face smiling. You already know the ears ringing is a *tell* alerting you to pay attention to what comes next. The symbol is the peppermint smell and the image of Grandpa Jake validates the first symbol. When you put these two symbols together, you would be able to discern that Grandpa Jake is near, likely enjoying the football game on T.V. with you (at this point, I'd probably strike up a conversation with him or just thank him for taking the time to drop by).

Hopefully, these two examples help illuminate ways in which spiritual symbols are given meaning. To the spiritualist devoted to gaining a deeper relationship with God, the process of identifying the language of Spirit is vital.

My suggestion is to keep a journal.

Creating your personal list of *tells* and symbols allows you to create a spiritual dictionary. Doing this is a powerful way to co-write your own language with the Holy Ones. This is life-changing when applied daily.

Commit to tuning in to the Divine and really listen to the promptings that present themselves daily. Make note of the *tells* you experience and pay attention to what happens next. List the symbols that follow and pay particular attention to patterns. Does a specific symbol associate only with a certain *tell*? Notice the meaning(s) behind the symbol (there may be more than one) and how it presents itself.

Remember, there are no coincidences...there is only the language of Spirit.

I REALLY DON'T HAVE TIME FOR THIS. WHY IS IT NECESSARY TO JOURNAL THIS STUFF?

Students take notes—at least those who wish to pass their courses do. They practice writing down the information they wish to retain. It's an eye-ear-hand thing that allows the human brain to remember.

Working with spiritual symbols is no different than learning to speak a foreign language. One can hear and perhaps converse a little, but to become fluent, one must become skilled with writing the language. This is because of the eye-ear-hand thing. Your ability to retain a foreign language increases as you practice writing down the words on paper.

The same is true for the spiritual language. The symbols have meaning at the moment, but without practice, these same spiritual symbols will often be forgotten or confused. Think about your dreams. How many dreams can you remember in detail if you fail to write them down. Now compare your ability to recall the meanings (ie: feelings, scents, colors, emotions, impressions, words, etc.) of the dream when recorded immediately upon awakening. The message is in the details!

No one said spiritual communication would be easy...but we all agree it will be worth it. Like committing to an exercise program (yikes!) to improve strength and endurance of the physical body, diligently listening to promptings, recognizing and recording symbols, and looking for pattern meanings will enhance your spiritual gifts.

Promise!

With diligence to journaling these things, you will find you've created a log of codes—spiritual language codes that have specific meanings for you.

This is how God will speak to you.

As you honor these symbols and learn how to interpret them, with time you will become a skilled spiritual communicator. This in itself is one of the greatest gifts from our Higher Power.

Trust me!

CHAPTER 11
Spiritual Sabotage

A sure-fire way to drop your connection with all things spiritual is to detour.

"What are you talking about?" you may ask. Well, this chapter is about spiritual mistakes and how to avoid them.

It's true that a few missteps can lead any would-be (and experienced) spiritualist down the bleak road to "no-go" with his Higher Power. In other words, there are deal-breakers out there that are sure to sabotage anyone's ability to connect with the Divine—few greater than distraction.

Several of these destructive deal-breakers (including a detailed list of distractions) are mentioned below, only as a reminder of what *not* to do when working toward a more spiritual relationship with the Holy Ones.

My hope is that this list is a nothing-burger for you—that you'll recognize its worth and already be at work eliminating these rather self-destructive habits. Doing so will allow spirituality to fill your life, open your understanding to the language of the Divine, and bring your insight.

With that...here's the list:

STUFF TO AVOID IN ORDER TO STAY CLOSE TO THE SPIRIT

Doubt and Denial – These "Double-D's" are twin mischief-makers when it comes to recognizing spiritual messages. Independently, they run interference with your impressions. Together, they wreak havoc with your belief in self.

Knowing that self-doubt can be one of the most destructive tools in the effort to build spirituality is a critical first step to its elimination. It's important that we dismiss self-doubt the moment it rears its ugly head.

Everyone struggles with doubting self, and especially doubting spiritual gifts as they come forward. This is normal. So, understanding that doubt is a natural part of learning to grow spiritually, allows us to be less judgmental of ourselves, and more forgiving overall, when we experience this type of deterrent.

Without exception, anyone seeking to understand and enhance spiritual gifts will experience doubt—doubt in the method one receives inspiration, doubt of the message received, doubt in ability, doubt in one's worth, doubt that the whole event was real! There's this book's title again—can you see the pattern?

Again, this is normal. But it doesn't have to be the "norm."

Recognizing doubt and choosing to step away from that doubt is the key. Let it go. Don't give doubt the power it seeks. Rather, choose faith instead—faith in self, faith in God, faith that this is real and happening to you. Step away from doubt and draw closer to the Spirit. That is the answer to dealing with doubt.

That is living with faith.

Fear – We all have it: fear of not being right about something, fear of embarrassment, fear of ridicule by those who believe differently, fear of misinterpretation, fear of not being "enough."

These fears are based in "possibility"—the stuff that hasn't happened yet. Most of the time, our anxiety is nervous energy about an expectation that never materializes. Even apprehension about something, like speaking in front of a crowd, comes from an expectation about the outcome. Most of the time, the events do not happen in the manner anticipated.

The adage: "It wasn't as bad as I thought" is common because so many people experience a different outcome than they imagined.

SO, HOW DO I KNOW THIS IS REAL?

Living in fear is living out of reality—dwelling in probability and imagination—not in the moment.

And that is the answer: Live in the moment.

When we pull our thoughts and emotions back to the "now," we step away from anxiety and fear. Of course, in the rare circumstance where life is threatened, fear is appropriate. The body responds and we kick into survival mode. But when our existence isn't threatened, which is most of the time, anxiety and fear does not serve us. Our body will still respond to a perceived threat even when no danger exists. This surges cortisol levels, raises blood pressure, increases heart rate, leads to inflammation, etc. The list of physiological effects goes on and on and on.

When we choose to live in that "middle way" taught by Buddha, we choose a different path and our bodies respond accordingly. Adopt an attitude of non-judgment to eliminate fear. Doing so will allow you to accept the spiritual gifts that present themselves to you. It allows you to release judgment of any situation and live in the moment—in a constant spiritual state of peace.

Comparison – "I'm not doing this right because she does it this way and I don't!"

How many times have you allowed this thought to enter your consciousness? If you're like most people, the answer is, "a lot!"

Think about the implication of the above statement. A comparison of self to another person takes the focus from the message we may be receiving and places that focus on another person. It's like having your telephone ring but answering your neighbor's phone instead.

A great lesson I learned as a young ER nurse taught me the truth behind focus. Let me share that with you.

As many know, the ER is chaotic, loud, and filled with lots of people and noises most don't often hear. Rooms are separated with curtains that do not filter out the unsettling sounds in an ER. In most cases, this adds to the chaos—especially for anyone inside the curtained cubicle. Most days, nurses have a patient load that pushes them to the edge. I called it "managed chaos." It's a challenge at best.

I had been an ER nurse for only a short time and was still learning the ropes. One particular day, my patient load was considered "easy"—the chief complaints were minor and none of my assignments were life-threatening. The job was to follow the protocols and doctors' orders for the patients then discharge them home. Easy-peasy!

Suddenly, down the hallway in the "Code" room, the cacophony of monitors alarming and concerned voices rose over the commotion of the rest of the Emergency Department. It caught my attention. I rushed out of one of my patient's room and headed to the "Code." Stepping inside, I watched as a chorus of medical professionals kicked into high gear, working in tandem to save a man's life.

For a new nurse, this was both exciting and terrifying. I wanted to join them.

"What can I do? Need help?" burst from my lips before I had time to think.

"Nope"

"Are you sure?" I couldn't stop myself and stepped closer to the man on the gurney to get a better look.

"Nope. We've got this."

I had been consummately dismissed. At least the nurse smiled when she said "Nope." Turning back to my "easy" patients I felt a twinge of rejection and a little resentment that I wasn't considered "good enough" to join in a Code.

As I stepped into my patient's room, I could see terror in her eyes. "Is that person okay?" she asked. Tears welled in her eyes and I immediately sensed that she felt afraid. *Will I be next?* was obviously her thought. My resentment dissipated into compassion as I looked into her teary eyes and smiled. I took her hand.

"That patient has a great team taking care of him...and I'm going to take good care of you."

SO, HOW DO I KNOW THIS IS REAL?

She smiled and relaxed. That moment, I learned a lesson that has never been forgotten in more than two decades. In that instant, I realized I could not be an effective nurse and be "excellent" for my patients if I kept my eye on the patient down the hallway.

This is powerful.

The same holds true for each of us as we work with the spiritual. Our gifts (to hear and listen to divinely inspired messages then share that information with those who wish to hear) will be lost if we focus on someone else's gifts.

Those who choose to listen and share spiritual messages have a calling. It's an assignment. Much like the assignment I had in the ER, the focus needs to be on those who need us and need our gifts. When we look at another's spiritual process, and compare ourselves to that person's methods, we cannot excel in our own.

Let me say that again: *When we compare ourselves to another's spiritual process and methods, we cannot excel in our own.*

Of course, learning from someone else is absolutely a must to gain experience. But there's a big difference between *comparing* one's self to another and *gaining education* from another's experience.

Without doubt, one of the greatest ways to improve our ability to recognize and receive spiritual promptings, and then share those to bless the lives of others, is to put on spiritual blinders and really focus on our own gifts.

Become that healer of souls who values and stays in the spiritual game—eyes on the prize and share blessings with those who seek answers.

Interference – Nothing is more irritating than white noise! This is particularly true when you're trying to tune into a particularly important radio broadcast or watch a favorite TV show. Interruptions in internet and phone service (mid-call especially) leaves everyone frustrated. I don't know of any well-liked interference (it's even a penalty call in a football game!).

So, if interference is a problem with the reception in our electronic lives, why shouldn't it also be a problem with our spiritual lives? I think it is. Only, the interference isn't quite as obvious as white noise or an interruption in technology.

Spiritual interruptions are subtle (just like the spiritual messages with which they interfere). Most of the time, we don't recognize what's happening. We don't often know that interference is cutting into our sanctity. But it blares and scratches and blocks our ability to hear the Holy Ones speak.

How does anyone recognize this kind of interference?

Sometimes, we can't. Most times, we must stop and go to stillness to realize our connection (with the Spirit) has been interrupted. When we stop and listen, we're able to clear through the distractions that can disunite a clear contact with the Spirit.

Often, this interference isn't even identifiable—these things come into our stillness as stealth as ninjas. But we can identify them once we recognize what they really are. Below is a brief list of some of the spiritual interference that invade our connection to the Spirit.

- **Emotions:** anxiety, depression, anger, and fear are just a few of the emotions that can cloud a clear connection with the Spirit. When we allow emotions to take control of our environment, for that moment, we abdicate our soul's association to all things spiritual. This happens because our focus is on the emotion. Changing our focus to an emotion also changes the energy behind our intentions. Doing so is akin to taking an offramp that leads to an unplanned destination. Our manifestations will alter along with the shift in our focus.

    Fortunately, we can always get back to our original destination, change direction, and re-manifest with new energy. Replacing distracting emotions with joy, love, and compassion for others builds the connection to spirit. This conscious shift brings the same compassionate energy and manifests joy, love, and abundance in our lives.

SO, HOW DO I KNOW THIS IS REAL?

Many may argue that joy, love, and compassion are also emotions, and they would be right. The difference lies in the focused energy behind that emotion (think of the physical body's response to each of these "positive" emotions versus its response to "negative" emotions). Anxiety and fear can be all-consuming, creating physical reactions that kick into a flight-or-fight state. Not a very pleasant way to feel, in my experience.

On the contrary, love and joy fills an individual with a sense of contentment. These sentiments take the physical into a state of peace, raising the cells' vibration to a higher frequency, calming the mind, breath, even the body's blood pressure and heart rate.

When we recognize that certain attitudes (and subsequent emotional reactions) can cause distractions that interfere with our connection to the Divine, we can take steps to keep our emotions in check. Noticing our body's response to how we feel about a situation is the tool to recognizing what's going on with our emotions and subsequent cell energy.

Consciously choosing to raise our emotional vibrations to maintain a spirit of peace brings us close to God. In this way, we open the channels that allow spiritual messages to flow.

- **Beliefs** – We all have them. Ingrained deeply within our souls, our belief system directs many of the attitudes and perceptions that color our world. These beliefs settle into the most internal part of our being, creating the base of our core values. Without realizing it, as we hold to these principles, we create the dogma that drives our actions, thoughts, attitudes, and judgement of the world around us.

  The choice to live in non-judgment and with acceptance (Buddha's "Middle Way") is still a value driven by a belief—the principle that this attitude or practice is "good for us" and something that would benefit self and others. These values drive actions. Benevolence is often the outcome. No one would argue that these types of beliefs bring an altruistic approach to living in this world and with others. I doubt anyone would object to this life path, either.

Of course, such benevolence would never include "doing for others" at one's own expense. In other words, self-sacrifice for altruistic means. We call this co-dependency. This self-depreciating behavior has also been labeled as "narcissistic martyrdom," a discussion for another time.

Again, intention is key.

Intention is behind differentiating the line between benevolence and anything else. Look carefully at your truest intention when acting on a benevolent impression. Doing so could be the difference between living in compassion (for self and others) and living with fear (of one's appearance in the eyes of others).

What you believe is behind your intention. Reflect on what benevolence looks like to you. Sit with the intention behind your actions and really look at your beliefs. Do your beliefs match your intention?

Beliefs are very personal and should not be assigned to you by anyone else. Because of the personal nature of each individual's core values, beliefs should be defined by only you and identified in the deepest stillness of the soul.

So, why is "beliefs" included in this section on distraction?

The problem arises when internal beliefs cloud our ability to "hear" spiritual messages.

Whether your upbringing included doctrine presented by an organized religion, moralities taught by parents, or principles learned independently through culture experience (or all of the above), ingrained within you is a set of ideologies that formed your basic core value system. As mentioned above, these values shape your beliefs—many of which you may not be aware of.

Internal "chatter" that suggests you may not be "good enough" or "smart enough" or "savvy enough" or "righteous enough" to hear spiritual messages always pulls the plug on spiritual input. Even worse is the belief that connecting with spirituality is "the devil's work." This topic is one that could be its own book. Suffice it to say that one person's method for connecting with the Divine is not necessarily another person's method. Again, this is very individual and extremely personal.

Spiritual processes are never right or wrong—they are just the spiritual dialogue that happens with God. This dialogue allows each of us to understand the messages that are sent intuitively. The exception would be when the intuitive "message" suggests harm to self or others (an action that goes against a basic core value inherent in human beings in general). To receive an intuitive "message" of harm is a red-flag that needs to be evaluated through a professional lens—a psychotherapist or medical expert in the field of mental and emotional illness. This topic has been written about by medical professionals with a much greater expertise than I. Should you be suffering from "messages" of harm, please contact an appropriate medical professional or go to the nearest Emergency Department for help.

For now, let's return to our discussion of the *process* of receiving intuition from a spiritual source that is in harmony with love, compassion, and peace.

History has shown mankind's response to assigning "right" or "wrong" to methods for connecting with God, and the resulting outcome for that assignment. A brief study of the Holy Wars or the Salem Witch trials gives a good example of this. When one's focus is on another's spirituality, he shifts away from his own. This is a distraction that happens frequently "in the name of all things holy." Disconnecting direct spiritual communication happens when that person (who views himself more righteous) judges another.

Think of the words of Jesus: "Judge not that ye be not judged." The powerful message behind His wise admonition is to stay on task, stay focused on God, keep your eye on your own spirituality, and turn from judging those who may be different than you.

Failure to follow this counsel disconnects our direct link to spirituality. Thankfully, this does not mean we cannot plug back in. We can always face this type of distraction, choose to avoid judgement, and let go. Literally, let Jesus take the wheel. That is the process for plugging back in to spiritual insight.

The trick is to identify the internal belief(s) that cuts the power to your connection.

Expectations – We all have them. It's difficult to get through a single day without holding an expectation about something. For example, when I brush my teeth with my particular brand of toothpaste, my expectation is that I'll taste wintergreen and my teeth with be clean. Last week, my husband ordered a taco salad with fries at the local drive thru. He expected to receive that order when he got to the pick-up window. In fact, his expectation that the order would be correct was so intense that he didn't check inside the bag until he got home. Unfortunately, his expectations were dashed when he discovered an enchilada something-or-other instead. Upset, he went back to the restaurant and explained the problem (that his expectations weren't met, and how dissatisfied he was with the outcome). Fortunately, they fixed the problem and my hubby enjoyed his meal, eventually.

Whenever we have expectations about a certain outcome, only to discover the outcome is different than that which we anticipated, we often experience disappointment. We then must adjust or correct the process to achieve the outcome we want. There is no judgment about this process being "good" or "bad"—it just is.

Accept or adjust. That's how it works with expectations.

The same is true for our spirituality. When we launch into a process with an expectation for a certain outcome, we may find ourselves faced with a completely different result. We must either adjust our process or accept that the result is what is "meant to be."

I am describing a different phenomenon than intention and manifesting (a process of surrender). Manifesting is an active practice—something we actively engage in *doing*. When we set an intention, we turn it over to a higher power and literally "let go," knowing that whatever comes forward will be in our best interest.

Expectation is a belief in a specific outcome.

An expectation that is specific and held "close to the vest," as it were, doesn't allow the Spirit to work miracles. Rather, we operate our process holding tightly to an outcome, and do so without flexibility. We've all experienced this and, most of the time, fear is behind the subsequent thoughts and actions. Letting go of an outcome is acting in faith—a belief that our Higher Power will take care of our wants and needs. Failure to let go creates tension (in our thoughts and our bodies) as we wait for something to happen. The connection to spiritual gifts becomes strained, brittle, and eventually breaks. Essentially, by clinging to what we *expect* to happen, we demonstrate a lack of faith—a lack of believing that God will pull through for us.

Let's take this truth to our pure intention to receive spiritual messages. We pray, meditate, listen, and wait for the answer. What is the expectation at this moment? Do we expect to literally hear spiritual promptings or see visions? Are we disappointed when that doesn't happen (ie: our expectations aren't met)? Consider a scenario in which the answer received comes in the form of a *knowing* or maybe the lyrics to a song. Do we have enough faith to recognize these messages as our "answer" or are we so rooted in an expectation that we fail to see the answer(s) as its presented?

An example of this happened to me many years ago during an exceptionally stressful time in my life. I had just finished a very traumatic 30 minutes in a courtroom, facing a hostile judge. She had just revoked my teenage kids' rights to make decisions regarding a very pressing issue. The decision put tremendous pressure on their school, sports, and many other activities in which they were engaged. In addition, there was a question of safety that this judge refused to address. I felt her decision was unfair and dangerous, and recognized the withdrawal of the judicial system to safeguard my children. I felt completely helpless to protect my children from harm.

This threw me into a desperate situation in which I needed some guidance. After immediately firing my attorney, I sat in my car and sobbed and prayed, begging God to just tell me what to do. It felt as if there were no options and I felt helpless as a mother—especially now that the courts had pulled away the kids' rights.

I figuratively threw my hands in the air and waved the "surrender" flag, giving up all control to my Higher Power. The situation was literally in God's hands. That moment, the answer came:

Go to Disneyland.

Say what?!

Go to Disneyland.

That wasn't the answer I had expected, and I was sure God had made a mistake. Disneyland was out of the question—we lived several states away and I didn't have two nickels to rub together (I was a single mother and dirt poor). So, I drove home and decided to solve my own problem since God wasn't paying attention. The search for a new attorney began immediately, and as I began to scroll through a list of local legal help, an advertisement popped up for travel nurses in California.

This got my attention.

The first job listed was less than 15 minutes from Disneyland. It was obvious that God, indeed, had been listening and that the answer was correct: *Go to Disneyland*. My expectation for a different answer had blocked my ability to hear the Divine. The outcome was very different than my expectation. As a result, I had missed it.

Thankfully, I finally dropped my expectations and followed the spiritual message I had received. I accepted a job at the hospital near Disneyland, taking my kids along with me. The rest is history

SO, HOW DO I KNOW THIS IS REAL?

(ultimately, a much better outcome than I had imagined). This was such a good lesson—one I've never forgotten.

When we fail to "let go and let God," we miss the messages. Channeling information from the Spirit will almost never come forward in a way we expect. Instead, the messages will come in the manner that provides the best outcome for us.

Remember, as you go forward in your communication with the Holy Ones, to let go of expectations and, instead, allow spiritual messages to flow however they are meant to flow. Receive without expectation and the information you receive will come in abundance.

Promise!

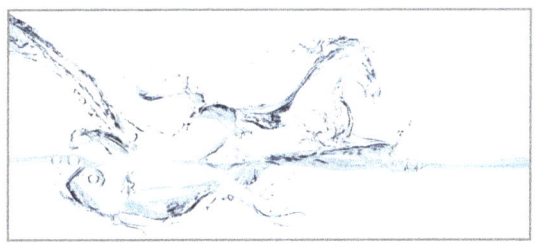

CHAPTER 12
So, now what do I do with this?

TRICK QUESTION?

Not really. You've just been given a roadmap to aid in your journey to recognizing and receiving greater spirituality in your life. What you decide to do with it is between you and Spirit. My hope is that you will ponder the concepts presented in this book and find a way to apply them into your daily life.

Spirituality is meant to bless us and bring us peace. Learning how to speak to our Higher Power is formidable and changes everything. With practice and faith, we gain the ability to draw on the All-Knowing at any time, receive direction, and then act in faith that we are being guided in all we do.

As you apply each of the topics discussed in this book, you will find your life evolve into more than just existence. You become a partner with the Holy Ones and a direct link to all things spiritual. People will recognize a change in you—some will celebrate as you evolve, others will turn away. All of this is "as it's meant to be."

Live in faith that God has taken you by the hand and is directing you along your path. Learn from the masters: Buddha, His Holiness the Dalai Lama, Kwan Yin, Jesus Christ, Saint Germain, and many others. Study and make notes of your own spiritual journey to better understand what your connection with Spirit looks like.

Above all, believe in yourself and your ability to receive and communicate with the Divine. Know who you are. Know your gifts. Hold them sacred and use them to build an abundant, peaceful, loving life. I know this is something you can achieve if you will only believe.

Hugs and Blessings ~
Marti

CHAPTER 13
Remote Viewing

WE HAVE ONE MORE TOPIC to discuss: Remote Viewing.

Why, exactly, did I choose to add this chapter at the end? It is because the ability to do remote viewing is not a "gift," per se, but rather, a parapsychological skill that can be learned by anyone. Granted, dedication and a willingness to study (and practice!) this skill is required to become successful as a remote viewer. But like any athlete, the degree to which you become accomplished in this skill depends on you. Without work and patience, one cannot expect to be skilled at anything, remote viewing included.

It's true that some people have prodigy talent. In music, these prodigies just seem to be born with an ability to command whatever instrument they elect to play. The same holds true with athletes. Some are "naturally gifted" and others become adept armchair athletes. While everyone can learn to throw a football, not everyone will become a pro quarterback.

The same is true with remote viewing (RV).

RV is a skill that everyone can learn. Many will choose to enjoy this tool from the safety of their immediate "life surroundings," while others will seek to expand their work—possibly aiding law enforcement, working on private cases, and/or assisting in public service. How someone chooses to use this skill is personal and totally acceptable, provided the intent behind its use is with love and benevolence.

Those who have heard me present this topic in public forums will know that I ascribe to the same remote viewing process utilized by the U. S. government, specifically the Star Gate military project from the 1970s. Without going into the history of Star Gate, a brief review of this operation will help explain my preferred approach to remote viewing.

During the 1970s, the DIA (Defense Intelligence Agency) created a secret program, its purpose to view and record data via psychoenergetics using "psychic spies." The CIA defines psychoenergetics as:

> "A mental process by which an individual perceives, communicates with, and/or perturbs characteristics of a designated target, person, or event remote in space and/or time from that individual." (*Project Star Gate*)

This process was adapted and trained to various, select individuals who had no experience with ESP or expressed psychic ability. In fact, it was reported that those without any spiritual gifts whatsoever were preferred RV candidates.

To gain a better understanding of what the definition of remote viewing and remote viewers meant, we refer again to the CIA:

> Remote viewing is "...the Acquisition and Description, by Mental Means, of Information Blocked from Ordinary Perception by Distance, Shield, or Time." (ibid)

From the Star Gate project perspective, the skill of remote viewing operates on set parameters that are strictly defined and monitored.

Targets are presented in a double or triple-blind scenario—meaning, the person giving the target reference numbers (usually latitude and longitude) does not know what the target is and/or the associated identifying numbers. Everyone is "blind" to the information that is given to the remote viewer.

SO, HOW DO I KNOW THIS IS REAL?

Once the remote viewer receives intuitive information based on the target identifier number, he records that information (impressions he senses) on paper. Often, the remote viewer(s) uses clay to sculpt the images seen. The medium used is less important than the information expressed artistically.

SO WHY IS THIS RELEVANT TO SPIRITUAL GIFTS?

Due to a bit of creative licensure, the skill of remote viewing fits into what I classify as "spiritual messages." Granted, the process is regimented and scientific, based on the Star Gate project protocols, but the viewer still experiences a spiritual phenomenon, with its accompanying sense of doubt, on occasion.

The question, "How do I know this is real?" is one that every remote viewer has asked himself.

I've included this chapter on remote viewing for those who show interest in this skill. Know that self-doubt and questioning (the validity of images "seen" by a remote viewer) will kill a remote viewing session as quickly as doubting messages sent from the Holy Ones.

Validation comes to a remote viewer after the test of faith—that the images shared by the remote viewer are of value (non-judgment) and given to him for a purpose. Sadly, validation does not always come to those who use other spiritual gifts, which can add to the self-doubt and disbelief. Spiritualists have their job cut out for them (a life lived in faith, hope, love, non-judgment, and on and on).

For those seeking more information about RV techniques, a few original sources from the Star Gate military project provide resources for training. Please be cautious of self-ascribed remote viewers who mistakenly use a psychic medium-type process to "view events." It's a fine line between psychic channeling and remote viewing. Research will help you discover which *feels* best to you.

In my opinion, remote viewing is best learned from professionals who have worked with the original Star Gate military project viewers. Course work, personal training, and educational material is widely available. Be sure to vet those who teach the skill of RV. In my opinion, only a few remaining experts (those who worked with Ingo Swann, Dr. Hal Puthoff, and Russell Targ's original program) remain. These highly experienced, unique viewers instruct on the process used by those who originated and created the label, "Remote Viewing."

I maintain that in order to get the purest training, it's best to go to the source (or at least as close as possible to the originators). Self-prescribed remote viewers, without proper training, are just that—self-prescribed without training. Ask yourself, would you submit to an operation done by a self-prescribed surgeon? Would you be a passenger in a jet flown by a self-prescribed pilot?

Me neither!

That is not to say that those without training have nothing to contribute, they absolutely do…we all do! However, for any work as important as remote viewing has been (consider the request to help find a missing person), using the skills acquired from a properly trained remote viewer is critical.

Again, the need dictates the level of training.

If you wish to learn remote viewing techniques to help you find lost keys or a missing cell phone, I don't think a certified course in remote viewing is necessary. However, if you feel the urge to assist law enforcement or work with others in an RV capacity, I would highly recommend investing in the proper training. You can find teachers linked to the Star Gate Project originators through a simple online search (or contact me and I'll guide you to the program where I received my training).

As with everything discussed in this book, your gifts (including the skill of remote viewing) are personal and meant to be uniquely yours. Stay in touch with your Higher Power. Meditate. Pray. Draw close to the Holy Ones so that your life can be blessed by all things spiritual. That is my prayer and intention for you.

SO, HOW DO I KNOW THIS IS REAL?

For more information about the author or to schedule a personal session, visit the website:

www.martirnadvisor.com

ABOUT THE AUTHOR

Marti Angeloni is a member of the International Remote Viewing Association (IRVA) with training received from the Remote Viewing Instructional Services, Inc. She works in Tacoma, WA providing personal Life Coach and Writing Mentorship services. She is a skilled medical intuitive and Reiki healer, with an RN background in emergency medicine in California and Utah.

Marti has authored books in the children's fantasy, historical fiction, supernatural, and paranormal genres respectively. Additionally, Marti is an award-winning screenwriter with several noted screenplays written alongside her writing partner.

Marti currently resides in the Seattle, Washington area.

For more information about Remote Viewing visit the International Remote Viewing Association (IRVA) at www.irva.org.

The personal experiences in this book **are not a guarantee** of what the reader should expect to occur for himself. The results may or may not be typical, and your results or experiences, if any, will vary. There is a risk that the reader will not experience events similar to those described in this book. All spiritual experience is personal. Again, whatever changes in your life that you make as a result of your journey is totally up to you based on your receptivity and personal needs, as determined by yourself and Spirit. I (the author) am not responsible for the outcomes you encounter. In writing this book, my hope is that the thoughts contained therein will motivate the reader to a joyful outlook and the consideration of potentiality on an individual and personal level.

Nothing is guaranteed. Everything is possible.

Marti

BIBLIOGRAPHY

Aikido. Retrieved August 19, 2019, from Wikipedia - https://en.wikipedia.org/wiki/Aikido

Psychologists Says Children With Past-Life Memories Exhibit PTSD Symptoms. (2014). Retrieved November 2018, from https://www.theepochtimes.com/psychologist-says-children-with-past-life-memories-exhibit-ptsd-symptoms_1113827.html

Merriam Webster. (2018). Retrieved November 23, 2018, from https://www.merriam-webster.com/words-at-play/sympathy-empathy-difference

Project Stargate. (2000) Retrieved December 2, 2019, from https://www.cia.gov/library/readingroom/docs/CIA-RDP96-00789R003300210001-2.pdf

The History of Remote Viewing. (date unknown) Retrieved December 3, 2019, from the

International Remote Viewing Association https://www.irva.org/remote-viewing/history.html

OTHER BOOKS FROM DOCE BLANT PUBLISHING

How to Spook Yourself Up
by Teresa Carol
An informative how-to manual for paranormal investigation.
https://doceblantstore.com/collections/metaphysical

Sullivan House
By A. M. Crane
Through blackened windows, the soul of the Sullivan House waits—dark, sinister, and alive.
https://doceblantstore.com/products/csullivan-house

NOTES

NOTES

NOTES

NOTES

NOTES

www.ingramcontent.com/pod-product-compliance
Lightning Source LLC
Chambersburg PA
CBHW071021080526
44587CB00015B/2451